MLB's Greatest Teams

LOS ANGELES DODGERS

Big Buddy Books
An Imprint of Abdo Publishing
abdopublishing.com

Katie Lajiness

abdopublishing.com

Published by Abdo Publishing, a division of ABDO, PO Box 398166, Minneapolis, Minnesota 55439. Copyright © 2019 by Abdo Consulting Group, Inc. International copyrights reserved in all countries. No part of this book may be reproduced in any form without written permission from the publisher. Big Buddy Books™ is a trademark and logo of Abdo Publishing.

Printed in the United States of America, North Mankato, Minnesota.
052018
092018

THIS BOOK CONTAINS
RECYCLED MATERIALS

Cover Photo: Ezra Shaw/Getty Images.
Interior Photos: 33ft/Depositphotos (p. 7); AP Images (pp. 11, 19, 22, 23); Doug Benc/Getty Images (p. 13); Ezra Shaw/Getty Images (p. 27); Harry How/Getty Images (p. 25); James P. Kerlin/AP Images (p. 22); Jamie Squire/Getty Images (p. 24); Jed Jacobsohn/Getty Images (pp. 21, 28); Jennifer Stewart/Getty Images (p. 25); Joe Scarnici/Getty Images (p. 17); Kevork Djansezian/Getty Images (pp. 5, 15); Mark Kolbe/Getty Images (p. 29); Stephen Dunn/Getty Images (p. 9).

Coordinating Series Editor: Tamara L. Britton
Graphic Design: Jenny Christensen

Library of Congress Control Number: 2017962672

Publisher's Cataloging-in-Publication Data

Names: Lajiness, Katie, author.
Title: Los Angeles Dodgers / by Katie Lajiness.
Description: Minneapolis, Minnesota : Abdo Publishing, 2019. | Series: MLB's greatest teams | Includes online resources and index.
Identifiers: ISBN 9781532115172 (lib.bdg.) | ISBN 9781532155895 (ebook)
Subjects: LCSH: Major League Baseball (Organization)--Juvenile literature. | Baseball teams--United States--History--Juvenile literature. | Los Angeles Dodgers (Baseball team)--Juvenile literature. | Sports teams--Juvenile literature.
Classification: DDC 796.35764--dc23

Contents

Major League Baseball

League Play

There are two leagues in MLB. They are the American League (AL) and the National League (NL). Each league has 15 teams and is split into three divisions. They are east, central, and west.

The Los Angeles Dodgers is one of 30 Major League Baseball (MLB) teams. The team plays in the National League West **Division**.

Throughout the season, all MLB teams play 162 games. The season begins in April and can continue until November.

The only MLB teams without a mascot are the Yankees, the Angels, and the Dodgers.

A Winning Team

The Dodgers team is from Los Angeles, California. The team's colors are Dodger blue and white.

The team has had good seasons and bad. But time and again, the Dodgers players have proven themselves. Let's see what makes the Dodgers one of MLB's greatest teams!

Fast Facts

HOME FIELD: Dodger Stadium

TEAM COLORS: Dodger blue and white

TEAM SONG: "I Love LA" by Randy Newman

PENNANTS: 23

WORLD SERIES TITLES: 1955, 1959, 1963, 1965, 1981, 1988

Dodger Stadium

In the beginning, the Dodgers played in seven different stadiums near New York City, New York. Then in 1958, the team moved to the West Coast. There it played in the Los Angeles Memorial Coliseum until 1961.

The next year, the Dodgers moved into Dodger Stadium. The team still plays there today. Dodger Stadium is the third-oldest ballpark still in use.

The San Francisco Giants are the Dodgers' biggest rival. This rivalry began in the late 1800s when both teams played in New York.

Then and Now

The Dodgers have one of the longest histories in MLB. Charles H. Byrne helped start the Brooklyn Baseball Club in 1883. The team joined the American Association a year later. Then it joined the NL in 1890. That is where it has played ever since.

The team has had different names over the years. It has been the Atlantics, the Grays, and the Trolley Dodgers. Finally in 1913, the team name officially became the Dodgers.

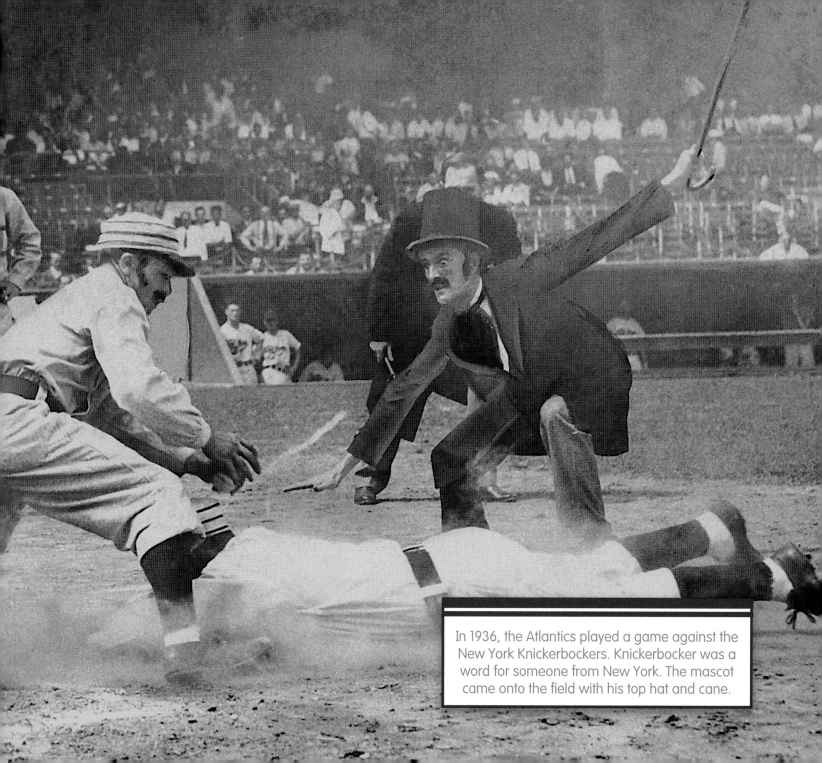

In 1936, the Atlantics played a game against the New York Knickerbockers. Knickerbocker was a word for someone from New York. The mascot came onto the field with his top hat and cane.

Dodgers President Walter O'Malley wanted to find a larger stadium for the team. But he could not find a big enough building in New York City. So O'Malley moved the Dodgers to Los Angeles in 1958.

The Dodgers played the Giants in their first game in Los Angeles. The Dodgers won in front of nearly 79,000 fans. Since then, the two teams have been rivals.

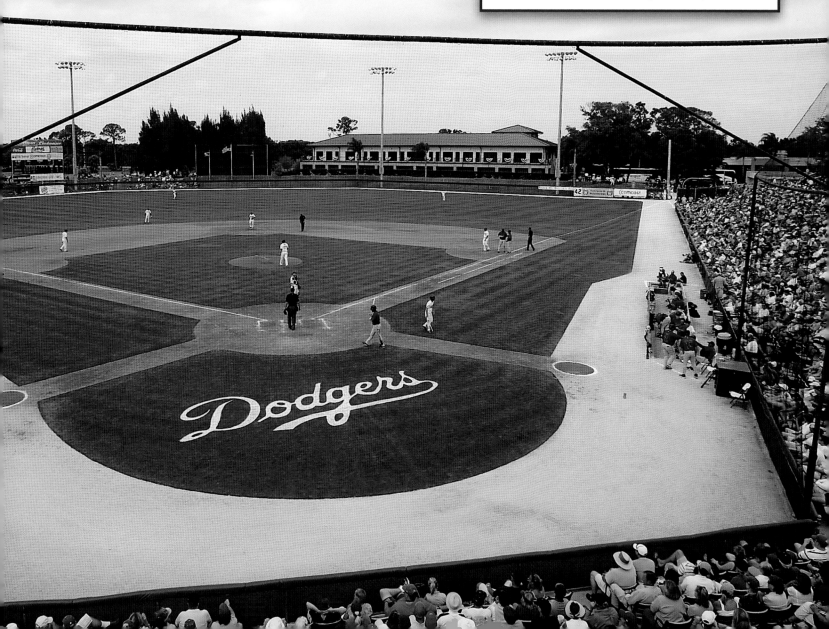

The Dodgers held spring training in Vero Beach, Florida, for more than 60 years. But the team moved to Glendale, Arizona, in 2009.

Highlights

Win or Go Home

The top team from each AL and NL division goes to the playoffs. Each league also sends one wild-card team. One team from the AL and one from the NL will win the pennant. The two pennant winners then go to the World Series!

In 1959, the Dodgers won their first **championship** after moving to Los Angeles. This was the team's fifth World Series during the 1950s.

The Dodgers' winning streak did not stop there. The team scored three NL **pennants** and won two World Series during the 1960s.

In 1962, players moved into Dodger Stadium. This new stadium could seat 56,000 fans.

Dodgers pitcher Sandy Koufax earned the 1960s Baseball Athlete of the Decade Award. This prize came after Koufax had won 24 other major awards during the 1960s.

In the 1970s, the Dodgers finished each season in third place or higher. And the team saw even more wins in the 1980s. Players took home World Series titles in 1981 and 1988.

The team did not earn any **championship** titles in the 1990s. But it did set a new club record for home runs in 2000. The team also won the NL West **Division** series in 2008 and in 2009.

The Dodgers played in their nineteenth World Series in 2017. The team lost to the Houston Astros four games to three.

Famous Managers

Walter Alston became the Dodgers manager in 1954. Under his direction, the Dodgers finished in second or better for seven straight seasons. He led the team to seven NL **pennants** and four World Series titles.

Alston managed more All-Star Games than any other MLB manager. He was with the Dodgers for 23 years. He **retired** in 1976. Alston was **inducted** into the National Baseball Hall of Fame in 1983.

Alston won the Associated Press Manager of the Year Award four times.

Tommy Lasorda became head coach in 1976. He led the Dodgers to two straight NL **championships**. And the team made it to the World Series in 1977 and 1978.

While with the Dodgers, Lasorda won 1,599 games. He also helped win four NL **pennants**, and two World Series titles. Lasorda managed the team until 1996. He was **inducted** into the National Baseball Hall of Fame in 1997.

Lasorda *(right)* managed the 2000 US Olympic baseball team. He led the team to a gold medal in Sydney, Australia.

Star Players

Jackie Robinson SECOND BASEMAN, #42

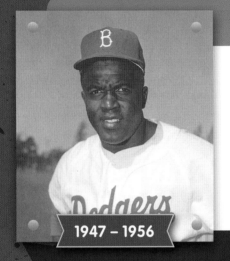

1947 – 1956

Jackie Robinson joined the Dodgers in 1947. He was the first African-American baseball player in MLB. He earned the NL **Most Valuable Player (MVP)** Award in 1949. Robinson joined the National Baseball Hall of Fame in 1962. In 1997, MLB **retired** his jersey number throughout both leagues.

Sandy Koufax PITCHER, #3

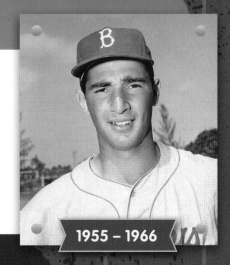

1955 – 1966

Sandy Koufax was the greatest left-handed pitcher of all time. He played for the Dodgers for 12 years. During that time, he pitched four no-hitters. He also earned three Cy Young Awards and two World Series MVP Awards. Koufax was named *Sports Illustrated* Favorite Athlete of the Twentieth Century in 1999.

Don Drysdale PITCHER, #53

Don Drysdale spent his entire **career** with the Dodgers. In 1962, he won the Cy Young Award for best pitcher in the league. Later, he pitched 58 straight innings in which the other teams did not score. Drysdale also pitched in five World Series. He was **inducted** into the National Baseball Hall of Fame in 1984.

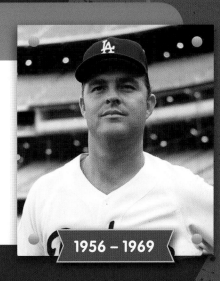

1956 – 1969

Ron Cey THIRD BASEMAN, #12

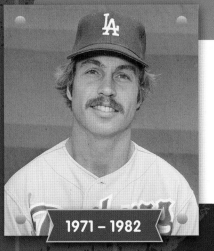

1971 – 1982

Ron Cey took part in six All-Star Games during his career. He played in the 1981 World Series. There, he led the team to four straight wins. Cey won the NL **Babe Ruth Award** for his efforts in those games. And, he earned the World Series **MVP** Award.

2008 –

Clayton Kershaw PITCHER, #22

Fans think Clayton Kershaw is similar to famous pitcher Sandy Koufax. Kershaw has played with the Dodgers his entire **career**. After ten seasons with the Dodgers, he has won three Cy Young Awards. And, he earned four NL pitching titles and the NL **MVP** Award.

Justin Turner THIRD BASEMAN, #10

Justin Turner began playing with the Dodgers in 2014. He has hit 71 home runs during his four-year career. While playing third base, he has made more than 700 assists. In 2016, Turner won the All-Star Final Vote contest with 20.8 million votes. So he won a spot in the 2016 All-Star Game.

2014 –

Corey Seager SHORTSTOP, #5

The Dodgers chose Corey Seager in the first round of the 2012 MLB **draft**. In 2016, he earned the NL **Rookie** of the Year Award. He was also involved in the 2016 All-Star Game. The same year, Seager took part in the Home Run Derby. There, he hit 15 home runs in four minutes and 30 seconds!

2015 –

Cody Bellinger FIRST BASEMAN, #35

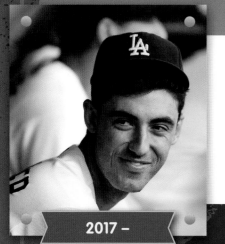

2017 –

Cody Bellinger began his **career** with the Dodgers in 2017. That May, he earned the NL Player of the Week Award. That same month, he won the NL Rookie of the Month Award. Later, Bellinger became the first rookie to hit ten home runs in ten games!

25

Final Call

The Dodgers have a long, rich history. The team has played in 21 World Series and won six.

Even during losing seasons, true fans have stuck by the team. Many believe the Dodgers will remain one of the greatest teams in MLB.

All-Stars

The best players from both leagues come together each year for the All-Star Game. This game does not count toward the regular season records. It is simply to celebrate the best players in MLB.

Actor Ashton Kutcher ran with the team flag before Game Six of the 2017 World Series.

Through the Years

1918
The MLB season ended a few weeks early. Some players had to leave to fight in **World War I**.

1980s
The Dodgers won 825 games during the 1980s. The team tied with the St. Louis Cardinals for most wins by an NL team.

1939
A Dodgers game appeared on television for the first time.

1994
Chan Ho Park made history as the first native South Korean player to be an MLB pitcher.

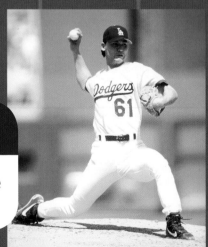

2001-2010

More than 3 million fans attended Dodgers games each season.

2004

MLB sold the Dodgers to California businessman Frank McCourt.

2013

The Dodgers began the year in last place. But the team finished the regular season in first place.

2010

Four Dodgers players took part in the All-Star Game.

2014

The Dodgers played its season opener in Sydney, Australia. The team beat the Arizona Diamondbacks, 3–1.

Glossary

Babe Ruth Award given to the MLB player with the best performance in the postseason.

career a period of time spent in a certain job.

championship a game, a match, or a race held to find a first-place winner.

division a number of teams grouped together in a sport for competitive purposes.

draft a system for professional sports teams to choose new players.

induct to officially introduce someone as a member.

Most Valuable Player (MVP) the player who contributes the most to his or her team's success.

pennant the prize that is awarded to the champions of the two MLB leagues each year.

retire to give up one's job, or to withdraw from use or service.

rookie a player who is new to the major leagues until he meets certain criteria.

World War I a war fought in Europe from 1914 to 1918.

Online Resources

Booklinks
NONFICTION NETWORK
FREE! ONLINE NONFICTION RESOURCES

To learn more about the Los Angeles Dodgers, visit **abdobooklinks.com**. These links are routinely monitored and updated to provide the most current information available.

Index